APR   2005

S0-BOF-899

Larkspur Library
400 Magnolia Avenue
Larkspur, CA 94939
(415) 927-5005

LEADERS OF
ANCIENT GREECE

ALEXANDER
THE GREAT

Macedonian
King and
Conqueror

LEADERS OF ANCIENT GREECE

ALEXANDER THE GREAT

Macedonian King and Conqueror

Bernard Randall

Published in 2004 by The Rosen Publishing Group, Inc.
29 East 21st Street, New York, NY 10010

Copyright © 2004 by The Rosen Publishing Group, Inc.

First Edition

All rights reserved. No part of this book may be reproduced
in any form without permission in writing from the
publisher, except by a reviewer.

Library of Congress Cataloging-in-Publication Data

Randall, Bernard.
Alexander the Great: Macedonian king and conqueror/
Bernard Randall.
   p. cm. — (Leaders of ancient Greece)
Includes bibliographical references and index.
ISBN 0-8239-3825-5
1. Alexander, the Great, 356–323 B.C. 2. Greece—History—
Macedonian Expansion, 359–323 B.C. 3. Generals—Greece—
Biography. 4. Greece—Kings and rulers—Biography.
I. Title. II. Series.
DF234 .R36 2003
938'.07'02—dc21

                                        2002007187

Manufactured in the United States of America

Contents

GREECE AND MACEDONIA
AT THE TIME OF ALEXANDER

BLACK SEA

THRACE

MACEDONIA

● **Sigeum**

● **Acanthus**

AEGEAN SEA

● **Phocaea**

● **Ephesus**

● **Chalcis**
● **Eritrea**

Delphi ● **Thebes** ●

● **Miletus**

● **Athens**

● **Corinth**

● **Halicarnassus**

PELOPONNESE

Olympia ● **Argos** ●

● **Sparta**

IONIAN SEA

CRETE

MEDITERRANEAN SEA

INTRODUCTION

Alexander the Great died at the age of only thirty-two in 323 BC. Yet in the thirteen years of his reign as King Alexander III of Macedon, he went from ruler of the leading state in Greece to conqueror of the biggest empire the world had ever known. He is called "the Great" mainly for his conquests and the military genius that made them possible. And yet there was more to him, for he was a huge personality. He believed himself to be the son of Zeus, the king of the Greek gods. The loyalty of his troops was based on their adoration for their king and general, for he fought alongside them in the fiercest of battles. Even when faced with the apparently impossible, Alexander achieved what he wanted to achieve as if by willpower alone.

Alexander, however, was not just the kind of man who stands

A second century BC sculpture of Alexander the Great, king of Macedonia

head and shoulders above those of his own time. He also changed the course of history. He made Egypt and the Middle East parts of the Greek world, and he initiated the spread of Greek ideas and philosophy far beyond Greece. Without the conquests of Alexander, it is hard to see how Christianity could have spread so easily in the first centuries after the birth and death of Christ, and the whole history of modern civilization would have been quite different.

However much historians might say "such-and-such was part of a trend," or "these things would have happened in much the same way even without so-and-so," it is clear that a few unique people have made such an impact on the course of human history that it is right to call them world-changers. Alexander III of Macedon was one such world-changer, and it is with very good reason that we call him Alexander the Great.

ANCIENT MACEDON

Although today there is a country called Greece, in ancient times it did not exist. Instead, there were many small independent city-states inhabited by Greek-speaking peoples. Some were no bigger than small towns with a little farmland around them. Others covered much larger areas, but by modern standards they were all small. Alexander the Great came from Macedon, a region now largely in northern Greece but also partly in Bulgaria and partly in the former Yugoslav republic of Macedonia. The Macedonians of the fourth century BC were on the edges of Greek civilization, both geographically and culturally. The Macedonian language was related to Greek, but Macedon's southern neighbors would not have understood it.

Whereas the Athenians governed themselves as a democracy, Macedon was still ruled by a type of monarchy that had disappeared from other Greek city-states centuries before. The oldest son of the king did not inherit the throne automatically. Instead, the army elected the new king. In practice, this meant approving the choice put forward by the leading landowners, known as *hetairoi*, of a candidate usually picked from one of the ruling families. Because of this arrangement, power struggles were common, and Macedon never managed to stay unified for very long. When a king was chosen, he theoretically had absolute power to govern as he wished. He was the commander of the army and owned all the gold, silver, and iron mines in the kingdom. However, in practice the king also relied on the approval of the hetairoi. He was in many ways the first among equals, and the hetairoi expected him to treat them with respect.

By the time of Alexander, classical Greek culture had influenced many aspects of the older Macedonian culture, but many old customs remained. The Macedonians were fond of heavy drinking and hunting. Many Greeks thought of the Macedonians as barbaric and uncivilized. The Macedonians no doubt looked down on the Greeks as weak and "bookish."

Macedonians and Greeks can be considered to comprise one cultural group when compared to other cultures, such as that of the Egyptians or Persians, but they thought of themselves as being distinct peoples in most respects. The culture that Greeks and Macedonians had in common and that spread throughout the empire Alexander conquered is called the Hellenistic culture. The name comes from another word for Greece ("Hellas") and the Greeks ("Hellenes").

SOURCES

For someone who had such an impact on his world, what we know of Alexander's life is clouded with uncertainty. Although several men who went on Alexander's campaigns with him wrote accounts of what happened at the time or very soon afterward, these original sources disappeared in the centuries that followed. All that we have available to us are the works of later writers, who used the original sources to produce their own versions of the life of Alexander.

The original sources were written by a variety of men. One was Callisthenes. It seems that his job was to be Alexander's "press agent," making sure when Alexander was away with the army that the people back home heard what the king wanted them to hear. Subsequent generations did not value his account, and he was known as a "flatterer." More popular was the account of Cleitarchus. He did not actually travel with Alexander, but he emphasized personalities and the more sensational episodes in Alexander's life. His was the tabloid version of history. More sober were the accounts of Ptolemy, who was one of Alexander's generals, and Aristobulus, who seems to have been an engineer. They were both favorable to Alexander, but even so they seem to be more accurate than Cleitarchus. Others who contributed to the literature on Alexander were Nearchus, one of his admirals, and Chares, who was a court official.

Unfortunately, none of these works survive now, over 2,000 years later. The earliest history of Alexander that has survived to our own day is that by Diodorus, who was writing nearly 300 years after the events he describes. He based his story on the account of Cleitarchus.

But Diodorus is not considered a very good historian. He was not very good at checking his information and he can be confusing to read, as if he himself did not really understand what he was writing about.

The Roman historian Plutarch wrote a biography of Alexander using a variety of sources. He was a much better writer than earlier historians, but he was a philosopher by nature, more interested in the personalities and moral qualities of his subjects than in giving a consistent and accurate historical account of what happened.

It was a Greek politician of the Roman Empire, Arrian, who wrote the best history from ancient times that survives today. He was clearly an intelligent man who understood far better than others how to write history. He based his account on those of Ptolemy and Aristobulus. Although Arrian's sources were biased in favor of Alexander, most modern accounts of Alexander's life and campaigns are based on Arrian's history. However, it is useful to compare Arrian's work with the other versions of Alexander's life to better understand Alexander's flaws. The best history is written by comparing different accounts.

Every modern account of Alexander is different from every other account, and each history focuses on different aspects of his career. Scholars disagree about many aspects of his life. This account aims to present a reasonably objective history of what is really known about him.

ALEXANDER'S EARLY LIFE

CHAPTER 1

2
3
4
5
6

Alexander was born in the summer of 356 BC, probably around July 20. His father was King Philip II of Macedon, and his mother was Olympias, a princess from a neighboring kingdom.

Olympias was a major influence on Alexander. Philip was away fighting his wars for long periods of Alexander's childhood, and he also had other wives. Any son of the king might inherit the throne, and so Olympias guarded Alexander's rights jealously. Her family was reputedly descended from Achilles, a great hero of Greek myth from the Trojan War, and she was also a worshiper of Dionysus, the god of wine, fertility, and physical and spiritual ecstasy. In the ancient Greek pantheon of gods, Apollo represented order and harmony, but Dionysus was his opposite, representing

King Philip II of Macedonia, father of Alexander. He succeeded his brother Peridicus to the throne in 359 BC.

wildness and lack of restraint.

In spite of his mother's concerns for her son, Alexander's position as the heir to the Macedonian throne was secure, and his father's affection for him was never in doubt. When Alexander was about twelve, Philip was given a fine black stallion named Bucephalas, which means "ox-head," but it seemed too wild and no one in the king's court was able to ride it. Just as the royal party was about to give up, Alexander said that he would tame the horse. He had noticed that the horse was startled by its own shadow. Alexander turned the horse to face the sun so that it could no longer see its shadow, calmed it down, and succeeded in riding it. Bucephalas became Alexander's favorite horse, and he would later ride Bucephalas in battle. Philip's pride and affection for his son were only increased by these examples of boldness and wiliness.

PHILIP II

Alexander's father, Philip, encouraged the influence of Greek culture in Macedon. Greek became the official language of the army and the government administration. Philip appointed Aristotle, the famous Greek philosopher, as Alexander's tutor between the ages of

A gold medallion depicting Olympias, Alexander's mother. She became the third wife of Philip II in 357 BC.

thirteen and sixteen. Aristotle's interests were encyclopedic, from philosophy and art to politics and science. It is clear that Alexander learned a lot from Aristotle, and when he invaded the Persian Empire, he took philosophers and scientists with him.

The fact that Philip admired Greek culture did not prevent him from coveting their lands

The philosopher Aristotle, whom King Philip appointed as Alexander's tutor when he reached the age of thirteen

and cities. After consolidating his power in Macedon and securing the borders, Philip turned his attention to Greece. In 340 BC, Philip went to war against some Greeks living on the border of Macedon, and he left Alexander, aged only sixteen, in charge at home. While Philip was away, a small tribe in northern Macedon revolted, and Alexander took control of the effort to stamp out the rebellion. The following year, Alexander accompanied his father on a major campaign into the lands north of Macedon.

It was in 338 BC that Alexander got his first taste of a full-scale battle. Philip had invaded Greece, and at Chaeronea the Macedonians met the army of an alliance of Greek states. Alexander was put in command of the cavalry, the most important part of the army. Philip's battle plan was superb, and Alexander played his part perfectly. The Macedonian victory was complete. The Greeks had little option but to submit to Philip, and he forced them to sign a treaty bringing them together in an organization known as the League of Corinth. Philip got himself elected president of the league and supreme general for the war he now planned to wage against the Persian Empire.

A silver coin worth four drachmas with a portrait of King Philip II, minted in 354 BC

THE MACEDONIAN ARMY

Philip had remodeled the Macedonian army so that it had become the most efficient fighting force of the time. The element of the army that made it so effective was the cavalry. Because stirrups had not yet been invented and men on horseback lacked the proper support for wielding heavy swords or accurately aiming bows, most cavalry units were armed with lances or javelins. They would ride to within range of the enemy, throw their weapons, and then gallop away before the enemy could catch them. The job of the cavalry was to harass and weaken enemy infantry, but in a frontal assault they could not be expected to break a unit of infantry if the foot soldiers kept their discipline and stood firm. Using their javelins as thrusting weapons, cavalry units could fight other mounted soldiers in hand-to-hand combat, but the infantry carried out most of the serious fighting.

Philip decided to make broader use of the Macedonian cavalry and to take advantage of their superior mobility. He trained his mounted troops to be superb horsemen who could control their horses and, most important, stay on them when fighting in close quarters. It was customary for units of infantry of this period to deploy in a dense rectangular block of men all facing the same way. This was called a phalanx. Effective as such a unit was, Philip realized that it was vulnerable if a highly mobile cavalry could outflank the phalanx and attack it from the side or rear.

It became the role of the Macedonian infantry to hold the enemy infantry in place long enough for the cavalry to ride around behind them. In order to do this, the infantry units formed a phalanx at least eight men deep, but sometimes there were as many as sixteen or thirty-two ranks of soldiers in the phalanx. The Macedonians used lances or pikes eighteen feet or more in length. This meant

A Thracian helmet and face mask. Thrace was a region in the northern Balkans that Philip II conquered in 342 BC.

that at least four spearpoints would protrude in front of the man in the front rank, each carried

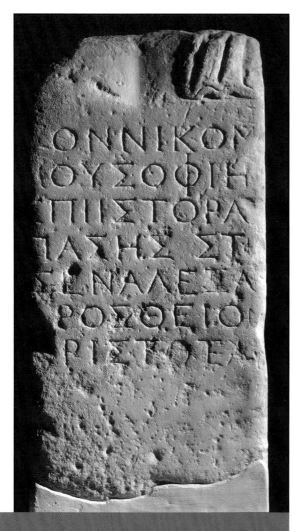

A stele, or stone tablet, commissioned by Alexander and dedicated to his tutor, Aristotle.

by a man behind him, making it much harder to break through the line. The Macedonian phalanx presented to the enemy a dense, porcupine-like mass of spears. By weight of numbers, the phalanx would either hold the enemy in place or slowly push them back. The key to this style of fighting was teamwork, and Philip made sure that his men were highly trained.

There were many other troops in the Macedonian army. Each nationality or group under Macedonian control had its own style of fighting. This variety was another source of strength because it meant that whatever the terrain and whatever the task, there were troops who could get the job done. But the coordinated use of infantry and cavalry and the tactics of pinning down enemy units and then outflanking or encircling them were innovations that would well serve an army on the offensive and that would create the foundation for a new type of mobile warfare.

ALEXANDER COMES TO THE THRONE

CHAPTER 2

Having gained control of Greece, Philip turned his attention to Asia. In 336 BC, Philip took time out from preparing his army to celebrate the marriage of his daughter Cleopatra to his brother-in-law Alexander, king of Epirus, a region on the border of Macedon. Alexander of Epirus was the brother of Olympias, Alexander's mother, and Cleopatra was her daughter. Philip invited special guests and dignitaries from all over Hellas. After the marriage ceremony, Philip walked into the theater for the celebrations, leaving his guards at a distance to show his confidence in the goodwill of his guests. One of his bodyguards, called Pausanias, rushed forward, pulled out a concealed dagger, and fatally stabbed Philip. Pausanias ran for a horse he had placed nearby, but he tripped and was killed by the other bodyguards.

The throne was now empty, and Philip's leading generals quickly declared their support for his son Alexander. This was partly because it had been clear that Philip wanted him as his heir and partly because of genuine regard for the young prince. The army elected Alexander as king at the age of just twenty.

Alexander had to deal with two problems before his grip on the throne became secure. His cousin Amyntas was also a serious candidate for the kingship. Amyntas was easily dealt with, however. Early in 335 BC, he was accused of treason for plotting against Alexander and executed. Whether he was in fact guilty is not known, but it was quite normal for rivals for the throne to be eliminated by whatever means were easiest.

More serious for Alexander was the suggestion that he had himself been involved in the murder of his father. If this charge was proved, the army might turn against him because Philip had been very popular. The person who had benefited most from Philip's death was, of course, Alexander, and there had been a very public rift between him and his father.

In 337 BC, Philip had married his sixth wife, also named Cleopatra, who was the niece and ward of one of his leading hetairoi, Attalus. Philip's other wives were now too old to have children, and he had only two sons, Alexander and Philip Arrhidaeus. Philip Arrhidaeus suffered learning difficulties, so the king wanted to make sure that there would be a fit heir to succeed him in case anything happened to Alexander. It seems that Olympias was jealous of this new and much younger wife. To make matters worse, Cleopatra was of Macedonian ancestry, whereas Olympias was a foreigner. At a drunken party, it was said, Attalus provoked Alexander by claiming that his niece would provide a pure-blooded Macedonian heir to the throne. Alexander threw his drink at Attalus, which enraged Philip so much that he drew his sword to attack Alexander. Fortunately for his son, Philip was so drunk that he tripped and fell, prompting Alexander to comment that the man who wished to cross from Europe into Asia could not cross from one chair to another. Whether or not the story is true, for some reason Alexander, most of his closest friends, and his mother Olympias went into temporary exile. They were soon recalled, however, and Alexander was back in favor at the time of Philip's murder.

The official version of events was that Pausanias had acted alone in killing Philip and that his motive had been that Attalus's servants had assaulted him and Philip had refused to punish Attalus. It seems very unlikely that Alexander was involved in the murder of his father, since that would have been the most religiously and

A gold medallion with a portrait of King Philip II

morally outrageous act he could commit, and Alexander was devoutly religious. However, it is possible that Olympias had encouraged some kind of plot against Philip because of her jealousy over Cleopatra. Whatever the truth of the matter, Alexander arranged for a grand funeral for Philip. In a purge both of Alexander's personal enemies

A small terra-cotta
sculpture of a woman
with an infant

and those suspected of treason against Philip, Attalus was killed and his niece Cleopatra was also eliminated, allegedly murdered by Olympias herself. The tomb of Philip has been found by archaeologists, and one of his wives is buried with him, almost certainly Cleopatra. By giving Cleopatra the burial of a queen, Alexander showed that he held no grudge, thus removing any lingering suspicions over the death of Philip.

Having come to the throne, Alexander intended to carry out the invasion of Asia that his father had planned. However, he had to secure his own position first. The Greeks had never been happy to be ruled from Macedon, and they threatened to revolt. But Alexander, with the swiftness that was to become characteristic of him, marched south so quickly that there was no time for the Greeks to organize any resistance. The Greeks had no option but to recognize the strength of Alexander's position and declare him president of the League of Corinth and supreme general, like his father before him.

The following year, Alexander took his army north to make sure that the borders of Macedon would not be threatened while he was away. In a brilliant campaign, he extended the Macedonian frontier to the Danube River. While he was away, there was a revolt in

A terra-cotta sculpture of two young women with string instruments

Greece, centered in the city of Thebes. Marching back into Greece, Alexander attacked Thebes and, in the massacre that followed, one-sixth of the population was killed. Alexander enforced the league rules about revolts, and the remaining inhabitants, some 30,000 men, women, and children, were sold into slavery. The Greeks learned their lesson and did not give Alexander any more serious trouble. With his position at home secure, Alexander was now ready to invade Asia. He appointed as his deputy Antipater, one of his father's ablest and most trusted generals. Antipater was to stay behind, watch over Macedon and Greece, and arrange for reinforcements to be sent out to Alexander when they were needed.

THE PERSIAN EMPIRE

At the time when Alexander decided to invade the Persian Empire, it covered almost the entire known world east of Macedon—modern-day Turkey, Syria, Lebanon, Jordan, Israel, Egypt, Iraq, Kuwait, Iran, and Afghanistan. The Persian Empire had been founded by Cyrus the Great in 549 BC when he usurped the throne of the empire of the Medes, who had themselves overrun the Assyrian Empire. The empire then began to extend its dominion over other peoples. A succession of empires had dominated the whole of the Middle East for centuries. This meant that the inhabitants were quite used to being ruled by foreign powers, and the most successful empires were the ones that allowed local peoples to enjoy their own cultures without interference.

This painting depicts an aerial view of a rebuilt Athens following the city's capture and destruction by King Xerxes of Persia in 480 BC.

The king of the Persian Empire was an absolute monarch. Even his most powerful subjects would sometimes refer to themselves as his slaves. Whatever the king commanded was done, and his status promoted absolute loyalty and obedience. The king ruled his empire through a system of local governors, known as *satraps*, who administered various geographical areas on his behalf. As long as the satraps sent the required amount of taxes and tribute to the capital, they were left to govern as they wished. There was also a fairly efficient secret service. Its main job was to keep watch over the satraps and other administrators to ensure that they did not plan a revolt. Because of its efficient administration, the empire experienced a half-century of peace, and because of the empire's vast natural resources, the king was immensely wealthy.

At the start of the fifth century BC, the Persians had attacked Greece, but with only limited success. In 490 BC, the army of Darius was defeated at Marathon. In 480 BC, another army under Xerxes captured Athens and destroyed most of its temples. An alliance of Greek states drove the Persians out, but the Greeks never forgot what happened. When Philip decided to try to unite the Greeks—under his own leadership,

A closer view of the reconstructed Acropolis in the center of Athens

of course—he used the excuse of the need to wage a war to punish the Persians. Alexander would undertake this war with spectacular results. After the successes of Philip, it must have seemed natural to Alexander to want to extend Macedonian power, and the wealth of the Persian Empire must have been another irresistible incentive.

THE CONQUEST OF ASIA MINOR

CHAPTER 3

Early in the spring of 334 BC, Alexander crossed into Asia at the head of his army. He had with him a force of around 32,000 infantry and 5,100 cavalry. Of the infantry, 12,000 were Macedonian pikemen, and an equal number were Greek infantrymen. Most of the remaining 8,000 infantry were archers. There were 1,800 Macedonian cavalry. The rest of the cavalry were from the Macedonian territories. Although the Macedonians were the elite forces, the whole army was well trained and well equipped. Alexander also had with him a number of experienced hetairoi, including a man named Parmenio.

The first thing that Alexander did was to visit the city of Troy in the northwestern corner of modern Turkey. This was the site of the exploits of his supposed ancestor Achilles in the war of the Greeks

A bronze bust of Hephaestion, a Macedonian general and Alexander's closest friend

against the Trojans. Alexander liked to compare himself to Achilles. It was said that Alexander slept with a copy of *The Iliad* under his pillow every night to remind him of what Achilles had done. At Troy, Alexander placed a wreath at the grave of Achilles, and his closest friend, Hephaestion, did the same at the tomb of Patroclus, who had been Achilles' closest friend.

Alexander also made sacrifices to the goddess Athene and dedicated his armor to her, leaving it in her temple. He received in return a shield that was supposed to have been left from the time of the Trojan War. If genuine, this shield would have been around 800 years old. Alexander had it carried into battle with him.

Darius III, the king of the Persian Empire, obviously did not feel very threatened by Alexander's invasion, for he left the defense of his territories to the local satraps. Alexander marched east with all his cavalry and the Macedonian infantry. At the Granicus River (the modern-day Kocabas), he encountered a Persian army.

According to Arrian, there were 20,000 Persian cavalry and an equal number of Greek mercenaries (soldiers for hire) in the Persian army. They had taken up a position on the far side of the Granicus, with the cavalry in a line in front and the Greek infantry behind. The river was fast-flowing and had steep banks—five yards high in some places. It looked impossible for the Macedonians, outnumbered as they were, to force their way across the river. Alexander nevertheless gave the order to attack, against the advice of Parmenio. He stationed most of the cavalry on the right, with himself in overall command. The phalanx of Macedonians was on the left, under the command of Parmenio.

One unit of Macedonian cavalry, whose commander was named Socrates, engaged the line of Persian cavalry while the rest of the Macedonian horsemen under Alexander carefully crossed the river. The Persians met Socrates' squadron with their best men, causing a number of casualties. At this point, Alexander observed a small gap in the Persian line. He charged into it at the head of his best cavalry. Alexander himself was the first to reach the top of the riverbank and the level ground above it. This was a dangerous moment for Alexander. The white plumes on his helmet were easily recognizable, and an elite unit of the Persian cavalry made straight for him. Alexander unseated their commander, Mithridates, a son-in-law of the Persian king, but then a Persian called Rhoesaces swung at him and cut off part of his helmet. Alexander ran Rhoesaces through with his lance, but now he was exposed, and Rhoesaces' brother, Spithridates, raised his sword to deliver a fatal blow. Just at that moment, Cleitus, one of Alexander's bodyguards, struck Spithridates so hard that he cut off his whole arm. Alexander was saved, but it had been a close call. By now, more of the Macedonians were reaching the top of the riverbank, and the infantry phalanx had begun to cross as well. Persian javelins were no match for the longer lances and pikes of the Macedonians, and the Persian cavalry soon turned and fled, leaving the Greek mercenaries behind them totally exposed. Surrounded, the Greek mercenaries were massacred. Only 2,000 were taken prisoner, to be sent as slaves to Macedon.

Alexander's first battle in Persian territory had nearly been his last, but he had won it through his own leadership and courage. Although the Persian commanders had made mistakes, such as forming two separate battle lines of cavalry and infantry so that only one could fight at a time, a less able general might not have managed to exploit these mistakes. With the Persians defeated, Alexander was able to take control of Asia Minor. There was little resistance as he marched south. Greeks inhabited most of these areas near the Aegean Sea, and they must have preferred to be ruled by a Macedonian rather than by a Persian. Indeed, Alexander treated them well, often excusing them from taxation. For the inhabitants of the non-Greek cities in the region, it was more a case of exchanging one ruler for another, with the same taxes to pay. Alexander was forced to besiege Miletus and Halicarnassus, two cities that refused to submit, but otherwise he simply stationed garrisons at key points to keep control over his newly conquered territory.

At the end of 334 BC, Alexander sent home for the winter any of his soldiers who had married immediately before the start of his invasion. This only increased his already immense popularity with the army. At the same time, he

A carving on the side of a sarcoph-agus of the Battle of Issus

continued to march through Asia Minor with the remainder of his army. He estab-lished secure lines of supply that enabled him to carry on campaigning throughout the winter, something that was almost unheard of in the ancient world. By the start of 333 BC, the whole southern and western coasts and much of the interior of Asia Minor were under Alexander's control. Alexander wanted to deprive the Persian fleet of safe ports in the eastern Mediterranean, since they would pose a real threat to his control of Greece. Although the Persian fleet had almost complete control of the seas, overall it proved unimportant in the coming war. To keep control

of the Persian Empire, Darius would make his main efforts on land.

In the spring of 333 BC, Alexander's army reassembled with reinforcements at Gordium in what is now central Turkey, ready to march farther into the Persian Empire. While there, Alexander went to visit the famous oxcart of the legendary King Gordius. The yoke for the oxen had been tied to a pole with a knot so complicated that it was impossible to see the ends. According to the legend, whoever managed to untie the Gordian knot would become king of Asia. Alexander tried to untie the knot but had no success, so he pulled the pole out of the knot instead. According to some accounts, he actually drew his sword and cut

A Roman mosaic depicting King Darius of Persia at the Battle of Issus

the knot. Alexander then declared that he would fulfill the legendary prophecy. We cannot know whether he believed this himself—after all, he had cheated—but it was certainly a great publicity stunt.

THE BATTLE OF ISSUS

From Gordium, Alexander marched through Asia Minor without resistance as far as the Cilician Gates, a narrow mountain pass.

Here the road was so narrow that a fully laden camel could not pass along it. If the defenders had stood firm, it would have been impossible for Alexander to force his way through. Fortunately for the Macedonians, the Persians fled as soon as Alexander approached. His reputation was working in his favor. The way now lay open to the prosperous city of Tarsus and the road down the coast to what are now Lebanon and Israel. The local satrap had no hope of stopping Alexander, so he planned

A Roman mosaic of Alexander at the Battle of Issus in 333 BC

A Roman mosaic of the Battle of Issus, based on an earlier Greek painting by Philoxenus in the fourth century BC

to plunder Tarsus before leaving. When Alexander heard of this, he galloped ahead of the army with a small force of cavalry. He covered nearly sixty miles in one day and managed to reach the city in time to save it.

Hot from the ride, Alexander jumped into the icy cold waters of the Cydnus River. Whether because of this, or because of fatigue, Alexander developed a serious fever, and his doctors feared for his life. One of his doctors, a friend since boyhood called Philip, produced a potion that he said would cure Alexander. Just as Alexander was about to drink it, a message arrived from Parmenio, warning him that Philip had been bribed by Darius to poison him. Alexander simply handed the message to Philip and drank the potion, demonstrating his trust in his friends and his lack of fear in the face of danger.

Alexander had reached Tarsus in the summer of 333 BC, and it was not until mid-October that he recovered completely from his illness. In the meantime, he sent Parmenio out to deal with any Persian forces in the immediate area and to consolidate his supply lines. When news reached Alexander that Darius had assembled an army at Sochi in Syria, he marched south to meet him. Having met up with Parmenio, Alexander left most of his sick and wounded soldiers and his heavy siege equipment at Issus and pressed forward to force a battle.

After a two-day march, Alexander discovered that he had made a serious and perhaps fatal miscalculation. While he had been heading south on the western side of a long mountain range, Darius had been marching north on the eastern side. The Persians had gotten behind Alexander. Darius captured, mutilated, and killed the Macedonians who had been left at Issus. Then he waited for Alexander to arrive. The situation looked bleak for Alexander. Darius had cut his supply lines, so he had to fight or starve. Yet Darius had a much bigger army in a good defensive position.

However, when Alexander arrived at the Pinarus River, behind which stood the Persian army, he saw that the situation was not as bad as it might have been. Between the sea and the mountains there was a coastal plain a little less than two miles wide, which meant that the Persians did not have enough room for all of their troops to deploy. Nevertheless, the river-banks were steep in places and would be difficult to climb. Boulders in the riverbed meant that horses trying to charge across it would be in danger of breaking their legs, so it would be up to the infantry to make the first attack.

The site of the Battle of Issus in present-day Turkey

Alexander put the Macedonian cavalry on the right and placed Parmenio in command of the remaining allied cavalry on the left. In the center was the infantry phalanx, with Alexander commanding the right wing. In all, Alexander had around 5,300 cavalry and 24,000 infantry. Darius is reported to have had 30,000 cavalry, an infantry force of 30,000 Greek mercenaries, and an additional 60,000 Persian infantry. Alexander was very heavily outnumbered. Darius put the majority of his cavalry on his right, facing Parmenio, with the intention of sweeping along the flat shoreline and breaking through to attack the left wing of the infantry phalanx. Darius himself took up a position in the center with his cavalry guards, behind the Greek mercenaries. On the left he placed some cavalry. Parmenio's job was crucial. He had to hold back the massed Persian cavalry long enough for the Macedonian right wing to break through the Persians in front of them.

On each side, the right wing took the initiative. The Persian cavalry put Parmenio under intense pressure, but because of the limited space, they could not make full use of their superior numbers. Alexander led his men across the river at a charge, and they succeeded in breaking through the Persian

An artist's conception of a Macedonian phalanx about to go into battle. Macedonian infantry used very long, bronze-tipped wooden spears, massed in front, that made them a formidable and terrifying force to oppose.

infantry. To his right, the Macedonian cavalry crossed the river, engaged the Persian cavalry to their front, and drove them back. The whole of the Persian left wing now collapsed. Joining his cavalry, Alexander charged left toward Darius, who turned and fled. Instead of pursuing him, Alexander carried on toward Parmenio's wing, where the

massed Persian cavalry, realizing that Darius had fled and that they were themselves in danger of being surrounded, also turned to flee. In the limited space, the vast numbers of Persian soldiers got in each other's way and were easy targets. The Macedonian victory was absolute. Although Alexander continued the pursuit until nightfall, Darius escaped into the mountains.

Again, poor tactics on the part of the Persians had helped Alexander, but he could not have won without the discipline and

Another artist's conception of what it must have been like for the enemy to confront a charging Macedonian phalanx

courage of his troops. In particular, Parmenio's leadership of the left wing must have been outstanding for his cavalry to have held out against such an overwhelming force. Alexander himself was an inspired leader, always in front of his troops and always setting an example of bravery for his men to follow.

After the battle, Alexander captured Darius's wife and children, who had been left behind in the Persian camp. They were valuable hostages, but Alexander treated them with great respect, as befitted members of a royal family. He assured them that Darius had not been killed, as they had supposed. Alexander also visited the wounded and presided over a grand funeral for the fallen.

THE SIEGE OF TYRE

Given the chance to march east into Persia itself, Alexander wisely chose to first consolidate his position by heading south along the Mediterranean coast as far as Egypt. Persia could wait, but the enemy fleet was still active in the Aegean Sea. Many of the Persians' ships came from ports along the coast, and if their homelands were captured, the Persians would lose their services. By taking control of the entire eastern Mediterranean, Alexander could completely deprive the Persian fleet of bases and finally take it out of the picture.

As Alexander marched south, the cities he came to all submitted without resistance. At Tyre, however, there was a snag. The inhabitants sent ambassadors offering to obey his orders. Alexander said that he wished to make a sacrifice to their chief god, Melkart. This was something only the king of Tyre was permitted to do, and so they refused him. Alexander decided to besiege Tyre. The task seemed impossible, which is why the Tyrians felt safe in defying Alexander. Their city lay on an island half a mile offshore and was protected by 150-foot-high walls. They had plenty of food and other supplies. They expected assistance from the Persian fleet, and they had their own small fleet that commanded the sea around the island.

Alexander ordered his men to build a 200-foot-wide causeway from the mainland to the island. As this causeway approached the island, the water got deeper, and the Tyrians used catapults to make the work impossible. The Macedonians built two 150-foot-high wooden towers and placed their own catapults on them. These were reported to be the highest siege towers ever used in the ancient world. They were dragged to the end of the causeway, where the Macedonians kept up a covering fire on the walls of Tyre, and the construction work continued. In a daring response, the Tyrians towed a ship to the end of the causeway and set it on fire, burning all the Macedonians' equipment and destroying the towers.

Alexander now began to make the causeway wider, and he brought up ships from the port cities that had surrendered to him. He now had more ships than the Tyrians, assembled from the very fleet that the Tyrians had expected to rescue them. The Tyrians blocked their own harbor and continued to resist.

Alexander tried to use siege weapons from his ships. The Tyrians swam underwater to cut the anchor ropes, until these were replaced with chains. The Tyrians lowered padding over the walls to protect them from catapults and threw huge boulders into the sea to prevent Alexander's ships from getting close to the wall. But whatever the Tyrians tried, there was no escape. Although unable to break through the wall at the causeway, Alexander's battering rams eventually broke through on the south side of the island. Bringing up two ships full of Macedonian infantry, Alexander was again in the thick of the fighting as his men forced their way into the city. At the same time, his fleet finally breached the harbor defenses. The Tyrians were slaughtered. The siege had taken seven months, and the Macedonians were in no mood to have pity on their opponents. The survivors, around 30,000 of them, were sold into slavery, and Alexander made lavish sacrifices to Melkart. The causeway Alexander constructed still exists as part of an isthmus linking Tyre, now called Sur, to the mainland.

Tyre fell in July 332 BC, and around this time, the Persian king, Darius, offered a peace proposal to Alexander. Darius offered a huge ransom for the return of his wife and children. He promised Alexander his daughter's hand in marriage, and he offered to surrender all his land east of the Euphrates River in exchange for a treaty of peace and friendship. The story is told that Parmenio told Alexander that he would accept these terms and end the war if he were Alexander. Alexander replied that if he were Parmenio, he would accept, but since he was Alexander he would not. Alexander's decision was perfectly reasonable. Darius was offering him little more territory than he already had taken, and certainly much less than he hoped to acquire.

ALEXANDER IN EGYPT

After taking Tyre, Alexander continued south, meeting resistance only at Gaza. There was another siege, and Alexander was himself badly injured by a catapult bolt that went through his shield and pierced his shoulder. Gaza was taken only when the siege engines that had been used at Tyre were brought down the coast.

From Gaza to Egypt, Alexander had to cross 140 miles of the Sinai Desert. As always, he took great care to make sure that his troops were properly supplied. The army followed a route along the coast, with the fleet carrying the heavy equipment and large supplies of freshwater. When he arrived in Egypt, Alexander met no resistance, for the Egyptians themselves had a history of opposing Persian rule. Alexander was proclaimed

A statue of Alexander as an Egyptian pharaoh, from Karnak

the new pharaoh, and he made sacrifices to the Egyptian gods.

And so, at the end of 332 BC, Alexander was ruler of all the eastern coasts of the Mediterranean, including the richest country of all in the Mediterranean, Egypt. The Persian fleet had nowhere to go and could no longer threaten the Macedonian forces. Alexander could now look east to Persia itself. But before continuing with his conquests, there were two things that he wanted to do. The first was to found a new city.

Alexander founded many cities in the course of his campaigns. Many of them were small places, just large enough to support a garrison and keep his lines of supply open. In these cities, he would often settle mercenaries who had come to the end of their contracts, or troops who had suffered injuries bad enough to prevent them from fighting in battle. Sometimes the aim of the city was to bring the native people of an area closer to civilization, giving them access to marketplaces and cultural benefits, and giving tax collectors access to them.

This city, however, was different. There was no need to control supply lines, and the locals were already highly civilized. This was to be a great trading port, and the site chosen had two superb natural harbors. Alexander personally marked out the streets and boundaries of the new city, chose where the temples would be, and decided which gods would be worshipped in them. Alexander named the city Alexandria, after himself. Alexandria was to become for a time the largest city in the ancient world. Alexandria was not only an incredibly wealthy center of trade, it was a center of intellectual and cultural development as well. It had a world-famous library. It was the place where Eratosthenes accurately measured the circumference of the earth. Here Hero invented the steam engine. Here the first book on algebra was written. And here many of the greatest theologians of early Christianity were based. Alexandria is most famous for its lighthouse, the Pharos, one of the Seven Wonders of the Ancient World.

THE VISIT TO SIWAH

The other thing that Alexander did in Egypt was to visit the renowned oracle of Ammon at Siwah with a small group of companions. This involved a 200-mile trek westward along the Mediterranean coast, and then south across the desert for a further 100 miles to the oasis of

A marble bust of Alexander, discovered in Alexandria

Siwah. Here there was a temple of Ammon, where the priest would take on the character of the god and answer questions with nods and gestures. When Alexander's party arrived, the priest welcomed the Macedonian king as the son of Ammon and led him inside the temple to ask his questions, leaving everyone else outside. When Alexander emerged, he declared that he was happy with the answers he had received, and the party left Siwah.

This is one of the most controversial episodes in Alexander's life, for we have no knowledge of what questions Alexander asked or what responses he got to them. Many of those who have written about him have speculated about his questions. Did he ask whether he was immortal? Or did he ask if he would conquer the rest of the Persian Empire? Did he want to know whether all of his father's murderers had been caught? Or was it merely that, as was usual when founding a city, he asked the nearest oracle whether the god looked kindly on the project?

Plutarch, in his biography of Alexander, quoted a letter supposedly written by Alexander to his mother, Olympias, which said that he had received secret replies that he would reveal only to her on his return home. It seems likely that this is genuine, in which case we can be fairly sure that no one else knew exactly what went on in the temple. If he would not tell his mother, he is hardly likely to have told anyone else. The fact that the priest of Ammon welcomed Alexander as the son of Ammon means little in itself, since this was no more than a proper way of greeting the new pharaoh.

Probably even before the visit to Siwah, Alexander came to believe that he was not the same as other men. His great successes on the battlefield seemed to confirm it. We know that Olympias encouraged the young Alexander to model himself on the heroes of Greek mythology, and this sense of greatness would have seemed natural to him given that he was supposedly

A carving of a Greek horseman hunting deer

descended from Achilles on his mother's side and Heracles on his father's side.

Later, Alexander would refer to himself as the son of Zeus (he apparently referred to Philip as his "so-called father"). Perhaps because the pharaoh had always been seen as the son of a god, he thought it right that he should be thought of as divine outside Egypt as well. At some point, the story was circulated that Olympias had been visited by Zeus in the form of a snake and had consequently conceived Alexander. We cannot know when this story was first put forward, but it is likely to have been after Alexander's visit to Siwah, and its origin may be in the fact that Olympias, as a worshiper of Dionysus, kept snakes.

THE BATTLE OF GAUGAMELA

In the summer of 331 BC, Alexander learned that Darius had assembled a new army at Babylon. The Macedonian commander returned to Tyre, made sure that everything was in order, and then marched east to meet Darius.

When Alexander reached the Euphrates River (in modern-day Iraq), Darius expected him to march along it toward the city of Babylon. Instead, Alexander crossed over and headed for the Tigris River, staying north of Darius. The reason is obvious enough. The wide floodplains of the Euphrates and Tigris Rivers are ideal for cavalry. Since Darius had far more cavalry than Alexander, the Macedonians sought to avoid giving the Persians an advantage. Each king hoped that the other would come to meet him where he wanted to fight. Darius's nerve cracked first, and he marched to meet Alexander. The fact that Alexander was conquering the territory in the north certainly influenced Darius's decision. Darius also had a far larger army to feed and pay for, and waiting was expensive. Although the terrain east of the Tigris was not suitable for the hit-and-run cavalry tactics that would have given Darius the edge, he managed to find a battlefield near Gaugamela with enough room for his cavalry to maneuver.

Having received reinforcements, Alexander had about 7,000 cavalry and 40,000 infantry at his disposal, including mercenaries. Darius, however, had some 35,000 to 40,000 cavalry and huge numbers of infantry. Ancient estimates range from 200,000 to 1,000,000 men, but even the lower figure is now considered an exaggeration. The Persian horsemen were good soldiers, but most of the infantry were not, and they played little part in the battle.

On September 30, 331 BC, Alexander arrived at Gaugamela with his army and established his bivouac early enough so that the soldiers were well rested. It seems that Darius kept his men standing in battle positions all night, perhaps fearing a surprise attack. The battle plans were much the same as at Issus. Darius hoped that his cavalry would break through on the right. Alexander was again relying on Parmenio to hold out while he himself tried to break through the Persian lines.

A coin featuring a portrait of Ptolemy I Soter, a friend of Alexander's and one of his generals. In 323 BC, he became satrap of Egypt and founded the Ptolemaic dynasty.

On October 1, Alexander led his men into battle. Unlike at Issus, because of the broad plain there was no protection for the flanks of his army, and the Macedonians were in danger of being surrounded. Alexander cleverly used this to his advantage by advancing diagonally to the right instead of straight ahead. In response, the Persians moved left in response to maintain their overlapping positions and, because they were less disciplined, a gap started to open in the Persian line. Alexander seized his moment and charged into the gap, forcing his way through. Parmenio led the resistance on the left. Alexander made for Darius's position behind the Persian frontline troops. Darius's soldiers temporarily stopped this daring assault, but Darius was in no mood to take any chances and fled the battlefield.

With their king no longer present, and faced with the threat of Alexander attacking them from behind after a breakthrough, the Persian army crumbled. Darius's lack of courage had betrayed him and he had fled before the battle was lost. Once again Alexander had won the day, and this time the heart of the Persian Empire lay open to him. Alexander again had to rely on the courage and discipline of his men. Nevertheless, the crucial factor was his superior generalship. He had devised a plan to win against the odds, and he had put that plan into action.

THE CONQUEST OF PERSIA

1
2
3
4
CHAPTER 5
6

For the first time, Alexander had himself publicly proclaimed "king of Asia." When he marched south to Babylon, the local satrap surrendered without a fight. The Babylonians had not enjoyed Persian rule. Xerxes, a previous king of the Persian Empire, had destroyed their main temple as punishment for a revolt. Alexander promised to rebuild the temple. He also reappointed the old satrap, a policy he followed throughout most of his newly conquered territory. None of Alexander's men knew the people of an area as well as the old satraps, who could therefore administer their regions more efficiently. As long as the reappointed satrap stayed loyal and collected the required taxes, this arrangement worked well. However, Alexander did leave a Macedonian or a Greek in command of the armed forces in each satrapy he conquered to make sure that security was not a problem.

After allowing his men some well-earned relaxation at Babylon, Alexander continued his progress toward Persia itself. He was joined by more reinforcements from Macedon and took the opportunity to reorganize his army. Persia and the lands to the east were mountainous and better suited to guerrilla tactics than full-scale battles. Alexander organized his troops into smaller, more mobile units, and changed their training program accordingly.

When Alexander arrived at Susa in mid-December 331 BC, the local satrap surrendered the city and its treasury—some 1,500 tons of silver—without a fight. Next, Alexander moved on toward the Persian winter capital, Persepolis (near modern-day Shiraz). On the way, he met resistance from a semicivilized hill tribe and the local satrap, who both tried to halt Alexander's progress through the mountain passes. In each case, Alexander showed the effectiveness of his army reorganization by taking his troops through the mountains quickly and surprising his opponents. Persepolis fell to Alexander and with it a further 3,500 tons of silver. Alexander stayed at Persepolis for about four months, consolidating his gains and arranging for the careful use of his newfound financial resources.

Near the beginning of May 330 BC, the vast complex of buildings that comprised the royal palace at Persepolis was burned down. According to Alexander's official story, this was the final act of revenge for the Persians' destruction of Athens 150 years before. It marked the change from the royal dynasty of Darius, whose palace it was, to that of Alexander. However, Alexander was by now following a policy of conciliation with his new subjects in Persia and the rest of Asia. He wished to be accepted as the next rightful king of the Persian Empire rather than the king of a foreign land who had conquered Asia. To destroy the palace hardly suggested that he was the proper successor to Darius. The story told by other writers was that at a drunken party Alexander was persuaded by an Athenian courtesan to burn down the palace because it would be popular back in Greece. But modern archaeological evidence suggests that the rooms had been cleared of valuable possessions before the fire, which certainly counts against any sudden and arbitrary decision to destroy the palace. We will never know the truth.

A vase painting showing Alexander on horseback chasing Darius of Persia, who is in a chariot

IN PURSUIT OF DARIUS

On learning that Darius had assembled a small army at Ecbatana (modern-day Hamadan), the Persian summer capital, and was awaiting reinforcements from the northeast, Alexander set off to catch him. It was essential for Alexander to take Darius out of the picture to make his own position absolutely secure. He hoped to take Darius alive and have him acknowledge the Macedonian king as the rightful ruler of Asia.

Darius hesitated, and then he retreated from Ecbatana. Alexander paused at Ecbatana to establish Parmenio as commander of this strategic city. Ecbatana was in many ways the nerve center of the empire and the key to supplying Alexander's campaigns further east.

Alexander pressed on after Darius. He took his troops, both cavalry and infantry, nearly 200 miles in eleven days in the hope of beating Darius through a mountain

A relief carving of Greeks and Persians in combat

pass. Discovering that Darius had gone through the pass already, Alexander waited five days to rest his men and horses. Moving through the pass, he advanced some sixty miles in two days along the edge of the desert now called the Dasht-e Kavir. When he

paused for the day to forage for food, he learned that Darius had been arrested by his own generals, so he set off on a final desperate chase. Traveling for two days and nights across the desert, he reached the camp where the forces with Darius had stopped the day before. Alexander learned from the locals that there was a quicker route to intercept the Persians, but it lay across a waterless part of the desert. Alexander took the toughest 500 of his men, mounted them on the remaining horses, and set off through the night. He had covered nearly forty-five miles when at dawn he saw the Persians ahead of him. Only sixty men had kept up with him, but Alexander attacked straight away. The Persians recognized the dreaded Alexander, stabbed Darius, and fled. When Alexander reached the wagon in which Darius lay, the Persian ruler was already dead.

Alexander had taken his men 250 miles in under a week, an extraordinary achievement for those times. Half the horses had died from the strain, and the rest were completely spent. But it had been in vain. Alexander took the body of Darius back to Persepolis and had him buried alongside his ancestors as befitted a king of Persia. It was July 330 BC, and little more than four years after invading it, Alexander was the indisputable ruler of the Persian Empire. He was only twenty-six years old.

THE CONQUEST OF THE NORTHEAST

A man named Bessus, one of the Persian generals who had arrested Darius, though not one of his killers, declared himself the new king of the Persian Empire and fled to the northeast (into modern-day Afghanistan) to raise an army. Alexander set off to subdue this region. Bessus lacked the resources to be a major threat, but he could not be allowed to threaten the stability of Alexander's newly won territories.

In such mountainous areas, it was impossible to decide matters in a single major battle. Instead, Alexander conducted a series of smaller campaigns that took three years. He moved his forces with his now legendary speed and split them up to fight on several fronts at once, entrusting parts of his army to experienced and loyal generals like Ptolemy and Coenus. Gradually, after many sieges of mountain fortresses and some setbacks, including more injuries to himself, Alexander gained mastery of the region. Bessus was betrayed to him and executed. Alexander made treaties with the various local rulers, who were allowed to keep their positions in return for paying tribute to him. Alexander also married Roxane, the daughter of one of these leaders, who was reckoned the most beautiful woman in Asia.

THE PHILOTAS CONSPIRACY

It was at the time of these campaigns that a plot against Alexander's life was revealed. A Macedonian called Dimnus was trying to find men to help him kill Alexander, and when a certain Cebalinus found out about it, he reported the matter to Philotas, the son of Parmenio and commander of the Macedonian cavalry. Philotas did nothing with the information because he thought it was false, and so Cebalinus got the information to Alexander through someone else. Alexander was furious when he found out what

The ruins of the royal council hall at Persepolis, the center of the Persian Empire, occupied by Alexander after the Battle of Gaugamela

had happened, and he accused Philotas of being part of the plot. When Alexander's guards attempted to arrest Dimnus, he killed himself, and so there was no way of finding out who was really involved. Since Philotas was unpopular with many of Alexander's

hetairoi because of his flamboyant behavior, they took this opportunity to turn against Alexander's boyhood friend. Alexander was persuaded of Philotas's guilt and had him executed.

Alexander knew that this would outrage Parmenio, whose other two sons had already been killed in Alexander's battles. Alexander may also have believed that Philotas would not have acted without his father's knowledge. With Parmenio in control of his financial reserves and a large army, Alexander could take no chances. A messenger was dispatched with great haste, and Parmenio was executed. With previous rumors of plots, Alexander had been much more trusting and tolerant. We cannot know why he had changed so much, but perhaps it was the corrupting effect of power. Alexander now split command of the Macedonian cavalry between his closest

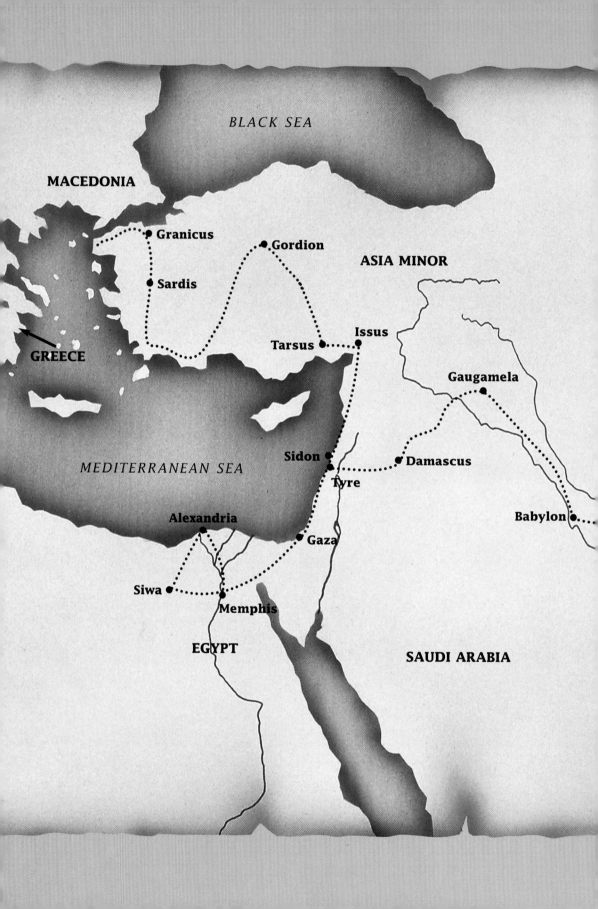

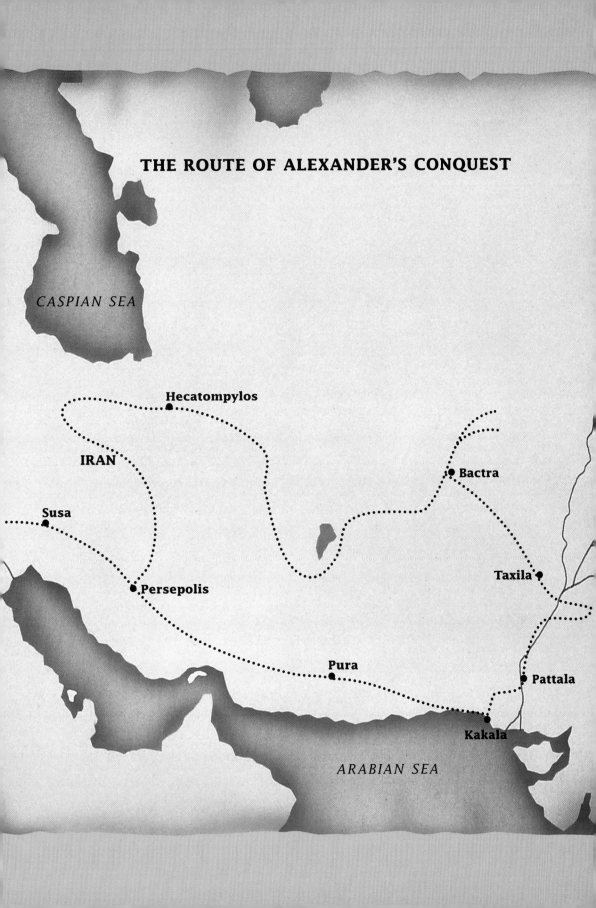

THE ROUTE OF ALEXANDER'S CONQUEST

CASPIAN SEA

Hecatompylos

IRAN

Bactra

Susa

Persepolis

Taxila

Pura

Pattala

Kakala

ARABIAN SEA

A marble carving on the side of a sarcophagus of a lion hunt

friend, Hephaestion, and Cleitus, who had saved his life at the Granicus River.

THE ADOPTION OF PERSIAN CUSTOMS

By now, Alexander was the ruler of a vast empire whose people were of many different ethnic groups. His generals were almost all

Macedonians, with a few Greeks. The satraps, however, were mostly Persians or other Asians. Alexander was also using troops from many parts of the empire. Many of his Macedonian troops were living with local women, even those who had wives back in Macedon. Alexander had founded numerous cities, bringing Hellenistic culture to every corner of the empire. For his people to live together in peace, it was necessary to combine all these different ethnic and cultural strands. Alexander started adding items of Persian clothing to his outfits, and he began eating Persian food. He had the sons of leading Asians educated in the Greek language and philosophy, and trained them to use Macedonian weapons.

Many of the leading Macedonians did not like this policy of cultural fusion. They saw the Persians as inferior to themselves, and they could not understand why Alexander treated them with respect. They were also alienated by the way that Alexander increasingly referred to himself as the son of Ammon instead of Philip. At one drunken banquet, the tension flared into tragedy. An argument started between Alexander and Cleitus over the treatment of the Macedonians in the army. They exchanged insults and nearly came to blows. As Ptolemy dragged Cleitus out of the room, Alexander called for his guards. When the guards, knowing this to be a harmless brawl, did not act, Alexander began to fear treason. Foolishly, Cleitus returned to the banquet. Alexander seized a spear from a guard and ran Cleitus through, killing him. When Alexander saw that Cleitus was unarmed and had not come back to kill him, he was filled with remorse and refused to eat or drink for three days. The incident seems to have had little effect on the loyalty of his followers, for such brawling was probably not uncommon and Cleitus had been foolish for coming back. Nevertheless, we can see the pressure Alexander was under.

THE END OF THE ROAD

At the start of 326 BC, having secured the northeastern part of his empire, Alexander arrived in the northern part of modern-day Pakistan intending to extend his territories farther than the Persians had done, beyond the Indus River. He knew that the local Indian rulers were too occupied with fighting each other to offer much resistance, and he planned to play them against each other. Alexander reached the Indus in May, crossed over into the kingdom of Taxiles, who surrendered to him, and then marched on toward the kingdom of Porus, who had failed to send ambassadors to welcome him.

Porus met Alexander at the Hydaspes River (now called the Jhelum) with a large army that included 200 war elephants. The river was too wide to ford, so Alexander and his men would have to cross on rafts. However, the horses would bolt when they smelled the elephants, making it impossible to keep them safely on the rafts. After mounting a number of attacks that were only feints, or mock attacks, meant to occupy the enemy, Alexander crossed unopposed about seventeen miles upstream and then marched south to meet Porus. Making superb use of his cavalry, Alexander totally outfought the Indians. When the Macedonian infantry advanced to deal with the elephants, their discipline paid off. They were able to pick off the mahouts, as the elephant drivers were called. The riderless elephants panicked and did more damage to the Indian troops than to the Macedonians.

Probably two-thirds of Porus's army was slaughtered in the rout that followed, and Porus himself was captured. When Alexander asked Porus how he wished to be treated, he replied, "Like a king." So Alexander gave Porus his kingdom back to rule on Alexander's behalf. With no army left, there was little danger of Porus revolting. Alexander's victory had been absolute, although shortly after the battle his beloved warhorse Bucephalas died of exhaustion and old age.

Alexander marched on toward the southwest, intending to conquer the rest of India, which he had believed to be quite a small country. But it was becoming apparent that India was a vast land and that there would be many armies to defeat. When Alexander reached the Hyphasis River (now the Beas), near modern-day Amritsar, he met an opponent he could not defeat—his own army.

Perhaps afraid of what they might meet in India, not knowing how far Alexander planned to advance, and weary from years of marching and fighting, the Macedonians had had enough. In a staff meeting, Coenus spoke out for the officers and men alike, giving their reasons for wanting to turn back. When this speech met with applause, Alexander must have known that he could not win. After three days shut up in his tent, Alexander made sacrifices to discover the omens and, declaring that the gods were unfavorable, gave the order to turn back. It was the summer of 326 BC. When Coenus died soon afterward, Alexander, who clearly did not hold a grudge against him for speaking up, gave him a splendid funeral.

THE RETURN TO PERSIA

Returning to the Indus River, Alexander sailed downstream and subdued all opposition on the way. It took nine months for him to conquer the Indus Valley and reach the sea, founding cities and building dockyards to promote trade along the way.

In one attack on a town, Alexander had been the first to scale the wall of the citadel, and he impetuously jumped down inside. Initially only three of his bodyguards managed to join him. He killed some of the defenders before being shot through the lung with an arrow. One of his guards covered his body with the sacred shield that Alexander had been given at Troy, until finally the rest of his men forced their way into the citadel and, believing Alexander to be fatally wounded, massacred the inhabitants.

When news reached the main camp that Alexander had apparently been killed, it was met with grief and despair. Even when a letter from Alexander was read out to say that he was

An artist's depiction of Alexander's troops attacking the war elephants of Porus, king of the Punjab, at the Hydaspes River in modern Pakistan

alive, the men did not believe it, thinking that the generals had composed it to keep up morale. As a river barge approached the camp, the soldiers saw Alexander's body lying on it, and their grief was deepened until he raised a hand to wave at them. A deafening cheer went up. On reaching the riverbank, Alexander insisted on mounting his horse and riding to his tent. As he dismounted, his men rushed to touch their king and brought garlands of flowers as a sign of their joy. They had revolted at the Hyphasis River, but their adoration of Alexander was undiminished.

When he reached the mouth of the Indus on the Arabian Sea in October 325 BC, Alexander arranged for his army's return to Persia. He sent Nearchus with the fleet to sail west along the coast and up through the Persian Gulf. This was to be a voyage of exploration of this previously uncharted coastline. Alexander himself chose to go by land with a small army across the desert of Gedrosia (modern-day Makran). He knew that he had to keep in contact with the fleet and help to supply it. So instead of the easier inland route, he kept close to the coast, marching mostly at night. Conditions were terrible, with no water for long stretches and supplies running dangerously low. The soldiers killed for food whatever baggage animals did not die from the heat, which at times was over 125° F (52° C). At one point, some scouts found a tiny amount of water and brought it to Alexander in a helmet. He poured it out onto the sand. All would drink or none, he declared.

A sculpture of a Macedonian war ship, with the warriors' shields stacked along the gunnels

The battered force finally made it to safety and joined up with the fleet and the rest of the army, which had taken the inland route. Alexander punished the local satraps who had failed to send him enough supplies while in Gedrosia. During 324 BC, Alexander progressed through the southern part of modern-day Iran, stamping out local resistance and making his way back to Susa and then on to Ecbatana. He replaced a number of satraps and generals who had abused their positions during the nearly five years since he had last been in Persia.

At Susa, Alexander arranged the marriage of many of his hetairoi to Persian brides, and he

A sarcophagus found at Sidon, featuring carvings of six mourners and, above, the funeral procession of a prince

recognized as legitimate the Asian wives and children of his Macedonian troops, giving them all wedding presents. He also paid off the debts of his troops. Then he arranged for any of his Macedonians who were too old or unfit for military service to return to Macedon with an honorable discharge. He planned to replace them with Persians trained in the

Macedonian style. This caused some discontent among the Macedonians, who felt they were being edged out. Nevertheless, Alexander continued his policy of cultural fusion throughout the army and the empire.

While at Ecbatana, Hephaestion, Alexander's dearest friend, died after a short illness, perhaps caused by a bout of heavy drinking. Alexander was grief-stricken. He ordered a funeral on a massive scale and laid plans for the building of a great step-pyramid in Hephaestion's honor.

FINAL PLANS

Early in 323 BC, Alexander traveled to Babylon to oversee the building of Hephaestion's pyramid and to lay plans for the invasion of Arabia. Alexander had ordered a great fleet to be constructed, planning to establish economic as well as political control of Arabia, a region with valuable resources and trade routes. During the preparations, Alexander held a banquet in honor of Nearchus, who was to command the fleet. A sequence of parties followed in the last few days of May, and Alexander began to suffer from a fever.

On May 31, Alexander had to be carried on a stretcher to make the sacrifices that he made every day, as was the duty of the king. Although his condition improved a little at first and he continued to give instructions for the Arabian expedition, by June 7 he had deteriorated again and was no longer able to make the sacrifices. Fearing that he was already dead, his troops pushed their way into the room where he lay. Unable to speak and barely able to raise his head, Alexander greeted his men with his eyes as they filed past. The men insisted on saying farewell to their beloved king and general, who had shared personally in both their hardships and triumphs. Toward the evening of June 10, 323 BC, Alexander III of Macedon, the king of Asia, died at the age of thirty-two.

Some have suggested that Alexander drank himself to death. Although he was capable of heavy drinking, something the Macedonians were renowned for, there are no grounds for suggesting he was a drunkard. Others believe that one or more of his generals poisoned him, perhaps upset by the policy of cultural fusion, but there is no evidence for such an idea. Most likely, Alexander died of malaria or something similar, his constitution weakened by the many injuries he had sustained over the years, especially the punctured lung he had suffered in India.

THE AFTERMATH

In Babylon, the Macedonian army elected Alexander's half-brother Philip Arrhidaeus as the new king. What followed was a struggle for power between Alexander's generals, who split the empire between themselves. Olympias murdered Philip Arrhidaeus and declared Alexander's son, born to Alexander's wife, Roxane, after his death, King Alexander IV. But Olympias had made too many enemies, and she and Alexander IV were soon murdered themselves. Antipater died in 319 BC after a short period in which he dominated the empire.

In a complicated series of civil wars, a threefold division of power eventually emerged. Macedon remained a separate kingdom under the rule of a dynasty started by Antigonus, who came

A third century BC marble bust of Alexander

from a prominent Macedonian family. Macedon eventually became a province of the Roman Empire in 146 BC. Most of Alexander's empire eventually came under the control of Seleucus, one of Alexander's lesser commanders. The Seleucid dynasty lasted for about 150 years before these territories finally broke up under pressure from Rome and the nomadic tribes from central Asia. The longest lasting successor kingdom was that of Ptolemy, who took control of Egypt. His last descendant was Cleopatra, from whom the Romans took Egypt in 30 BC.

In a dozen years, Alexander had changed the face of the known world. Hellenistic culture spread as far as Afghanistan. Alexander had tried to create a world of different cultures and ethnic groups living in harmony. It was at Alexandria in particular that Hellenistic culture was preserved and enriched, eventually becoming the medium for the spread of Christianity and the foundation of modern Western society.

GLOSSARY

Achilles A hero from Greek mythology. The only place he could be injured was in his heel (hence the expression "Achilles' heel," meaning "weak spot"). He was the mightiest warrior in the Trojan War, which is the subject of Homer's epic poem *The Iliad*.

Ammon The king of the gods in Egyptian mythology. The Greeks usually regarded him as being the same as their god Zeus.

Dionysus A Greek god. He was the son of Zeus. Dionysus was the god of wine, the theater, and ecstatic experience.

Heracles The greatest of the heroes in Greek mythology. He was the son of Zeus, famous for his strength and bravery. People throughout the Hellenistic world worshiped him.

hetairoi The name given to the wealthy and powerful landowners who acted as Macedon's senators.

oracle In Greek mythology, humans were able to seek the advice of a god through an oracle. Usually this involved the god speaking through a priest or priestess. The most famous and reliable oracles were those of Apollo at Delphi, Zeus at Dodona, and Zeus-Ammon at Siwah.

Persia The region of Persia, now in modern-day Iran, was only one part of the whole Persian Empire. The king was an ethnic Persian, as were most of his satraps.

phalanx An infantry formation relying on strength in numbers, with each man fighting as a disciplined member of a team rather than as an individual.

satrap The governor of a province (satrapy) in the Persian Empire. He had full authority in both civil and military matters, and was responsible for supplying troops and taxes to the king.

Zeus The king of the gods in Greek mythology. He was the god of weather and especially thunder, but he also had many other responsibilities.

For More Information

American Classical League
Miami University
Oxford, OH 45056
e-mail: info@aclclassics.org
Web site: http://www.aclclassics.org

The Classical Association
Room 323, Third Floor
Senate House
London WC1E 7HU
England
+ 44 20-7862-8706
e-mail: Clare.Roberts@sas.ac.uk
Web site: http://www.sas.ac.uk/icls/
    classass

International Plutarch Society
Department of History
Utah State University
0710 Old Main Hill
Logan, UT 84322-0710
Web site: http://www.usu.edu/history/
    plout.htm

National Junior Classical League
Miami University
Oxford, OH 45056-1694
(513) 529-7741
Web site: http://www.njcl.org

WEB SITES

Due to the changing nature of Internet links, the Rosen Publishing Group, Inc., has developed an online list of Web sites related to the subject of this book. This site is updated regularly. Please use this link to access the list:

http://www.rosenlinks.com/lag/algr/

For Further Reading

Briant, Pierre. *Alexander the Great.* London: Thames and Hudson, Ltd., 1996.

Chrisp, Peter. *Alexander the Great* (DK Discoveries). London: Penguin Books, Ltd., 2000.

Green, Peter. *Alexander of Macedon 356–323 BC: A Historical Biography.* Berkeley, CA: University Presses of California, 1992.

Langley, Andrew. *Alexander the Great: The Greatest Ruler of the Ancient World.* Oxford, England: Oxford University Press, 1998.

Wood, Michael. *In the Footsteps of Alexander the Great.* London: BBC Consumer Publishing, 2001.

BIBLIOGRAPHY

Arrian. *Alexander the Great. Selections from Arrian.* Translated by J.G. Lloyd. New York: Cambridge University Press, 1981.

Hamilton, J. *Alexander the Great.* London: Hutchinson University Library, 1973.

Hammond, Nicholas. *Alexander the Great: King, Commander and Statesman.* Bristol, England: The Bristol Press, 1989.

Plutarch. *The Age of Alexander: Nine Greek Lives.* Translated by Ian Scott-Kilvert. New York: Viking-Penguin, 1977.

Roisman, Joseph, ed. *Alexander the Great: Ancient and Modern Perspectives.* Lexington, KY: D.C. Heath and Co., 1995.

Index

ABOUT THE AUTHOR

Bernard Randall read ancient history and philosophy at St. Andrew's University, Scotland, before moving to the University of Edinburgh, Scotland, for a master's degree in classics. He is shortly to complete his doctorate on fifth century BC Greece at the University of Manchester, England. He has taught Greek and Roman history at the University of Manchester, and Greek history for the Open University since 2000. His main research interest is the history of Sparta up to 400 BC. His other interests include early church history and theology, rugby, the Discworld novels of Terry Pratchett, and juggling.

CREDITS

PHOTO CREDITS

Cover, pp. 32–33, 35, 52–53, 54–55, 90–91 © AKG/Peter Connolly; cover inset, pp. 3, 27, 44, 45, 46–47, 64 © AKG London; pp. 8, 21, 28, 30, 42–43, 66, 69, 84–85, 93, 94–95, 98 © AKG London/Erich Lessing; p. 16 © Chiaramorti Museum, Vatican/ Dagli Orti/The Art Archive; p. 17 © Archaeological Museum, Salonica/Dagli Orti/The Art Archive; p. 18 © Museo Nationale Romano, Rome/Dagli Orti/The Art Archive; p. 19 © Dagli Orti/The Art Archive; p. 22 © Epigraphical Museum, Athens/Dagli Orti/The Art Archive; p. 38 © The Art Archive/Museo del Prado, Madrid/Dagli Orti; p. 50 © Jane Taylor/Sonia Halliday Photographs; p. 61 © Egyptian Museum, Cairo/ Dagli Orti/The Art Archive; pp. 74–75 © Archaeological

Museum, Naples/Dagli Orti/The Art Archive; pp. 76–77 © Archaeological Museum, Istanbul/ Dagli Orti/The Art Archive; pp. 80–81 © T. C. Rising/Sonia Halliday Photographs.

EDITOR

Jake Goldberg

DESIGN

Evelyn Horovicz

CITY OF LARKSPUR LIBRARY